LIVES AND DIES

DAVID MILLER

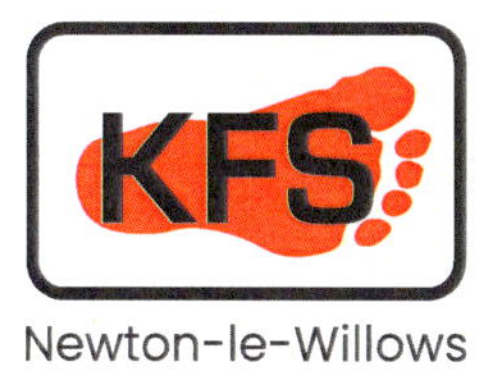

Newton-le-Willows

Published in the United Kingdom in 2025
by The Knives Forks And Spoons Press,
51 Pipit Avenue,
Newton-le-Willows,
Merseyside,
WA12 9RG.

ISBN 978-1-916590-18-2

Acknowledgements:

This book consists of a single poem and a series of ink paintings on paper, sometimes including collage and/or pencil. The poem has been published in *Tears in the Fence.*

Everything herein was created after the death of my wife Dodo (the philosopher Doreen Maitre) in June 2022; along with much else that I've written and painted. Grief and sorrow are the touchstones. This book is dedicated to her memory, with love.

Other deaths have occurred and been significant, such as the poet and anthropologist Tom Lowenstein's.

– DM

– May 2025

LIVES AND DIES

Contents

LIVES AND DIES

Lives and Dies

The peacock angel
lives

in every ethical act.
The peacock angel

dies
in every ethical act.

Does the peacock angel
live then die

or die then live?
In each

and every ethical act
eternally.

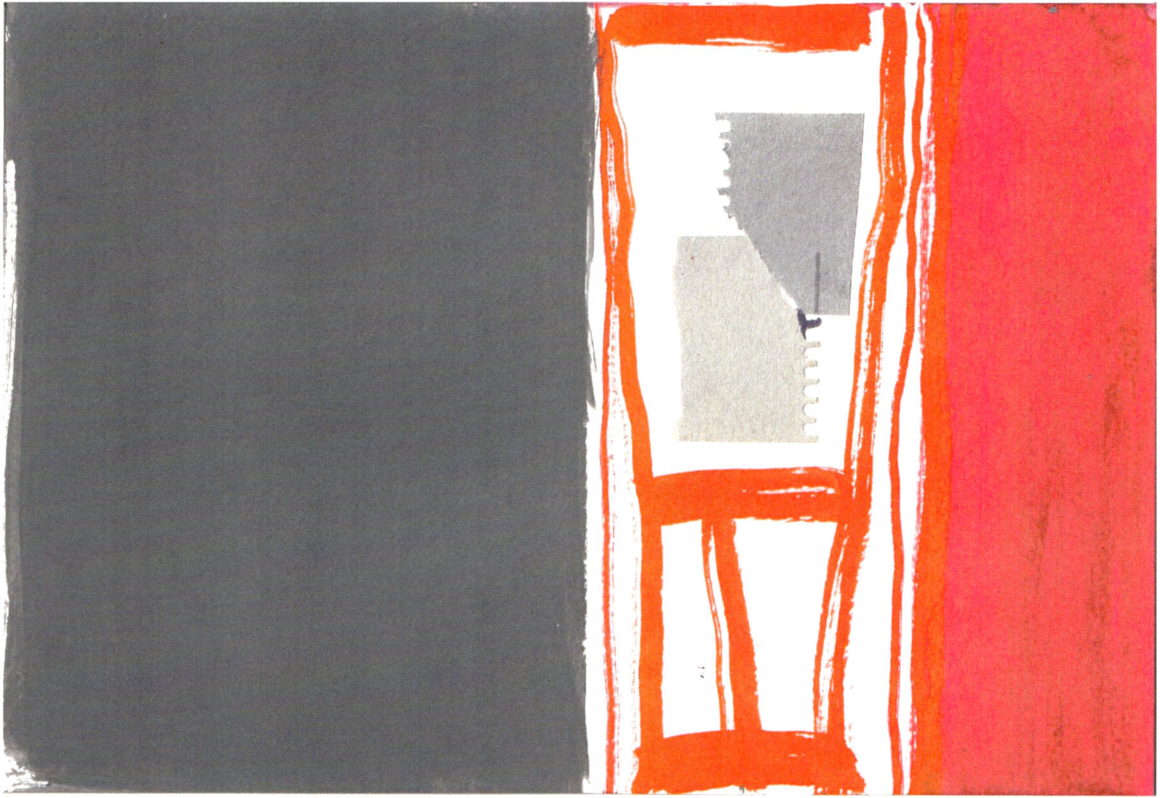

ink & collage (from grey to pink)

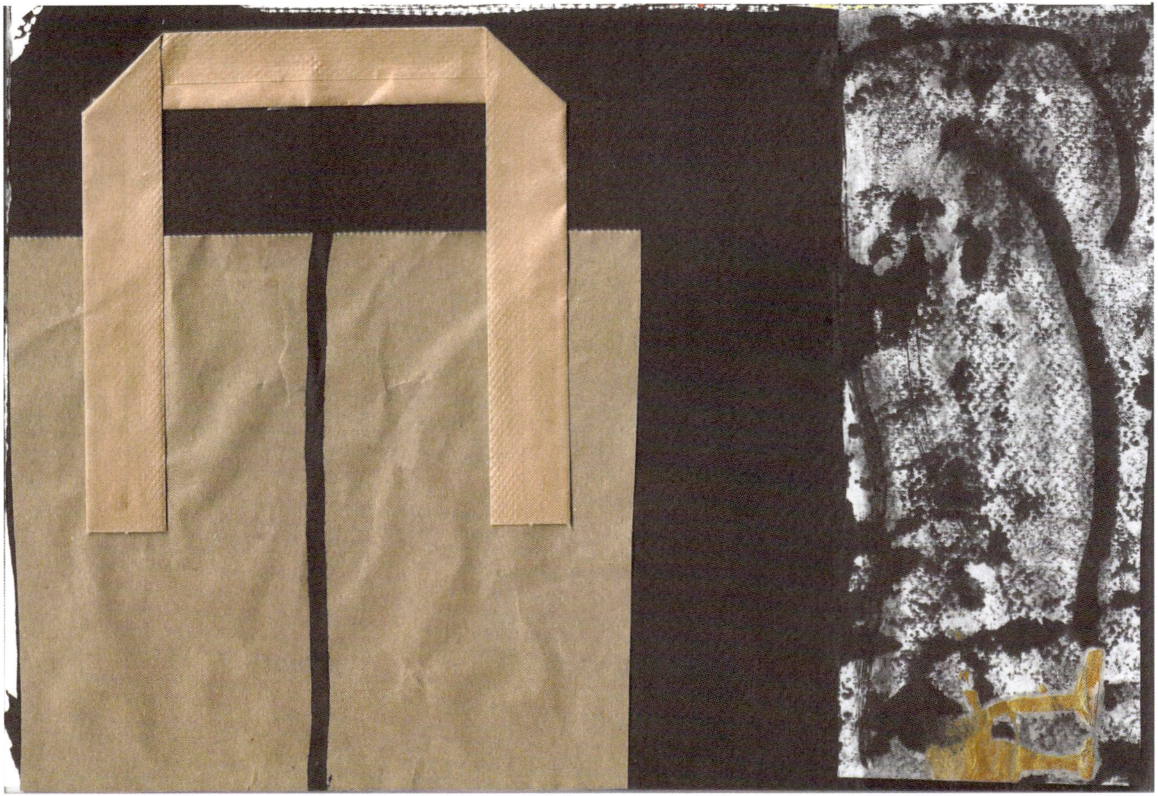

 | ink & collage (for Tapies)

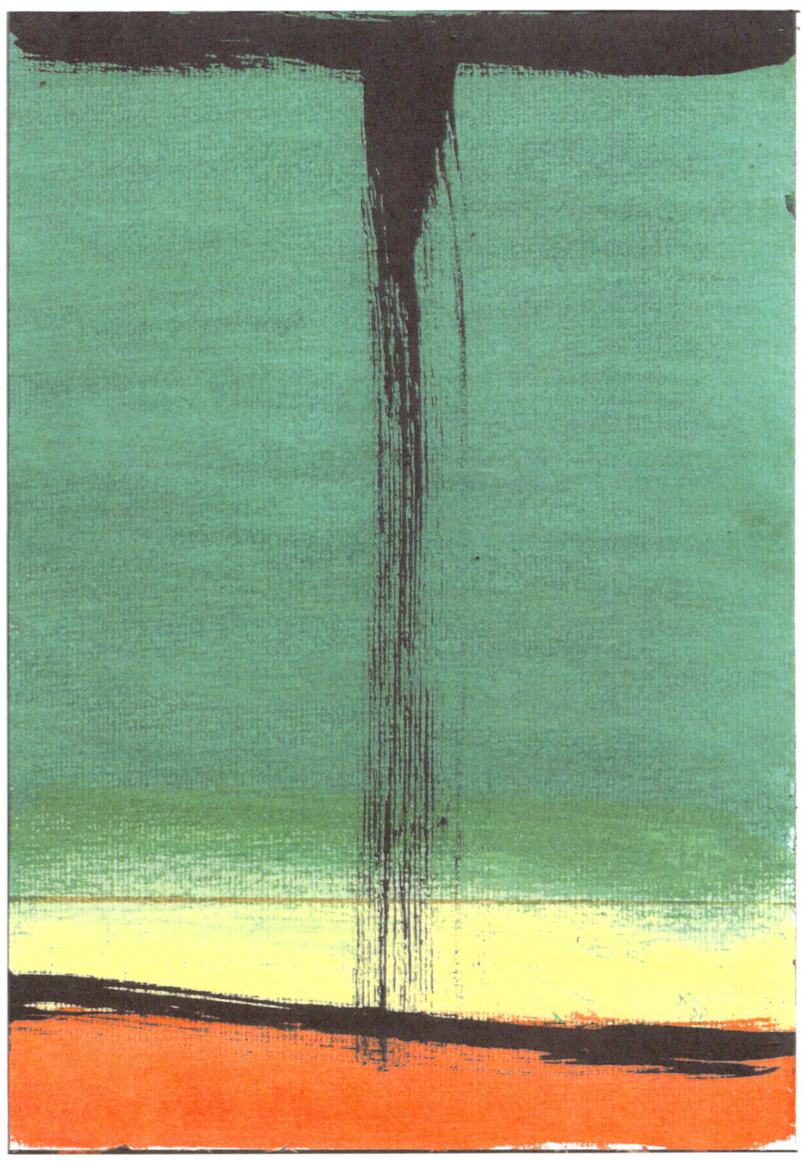

ink & pencil (Amsterdam)

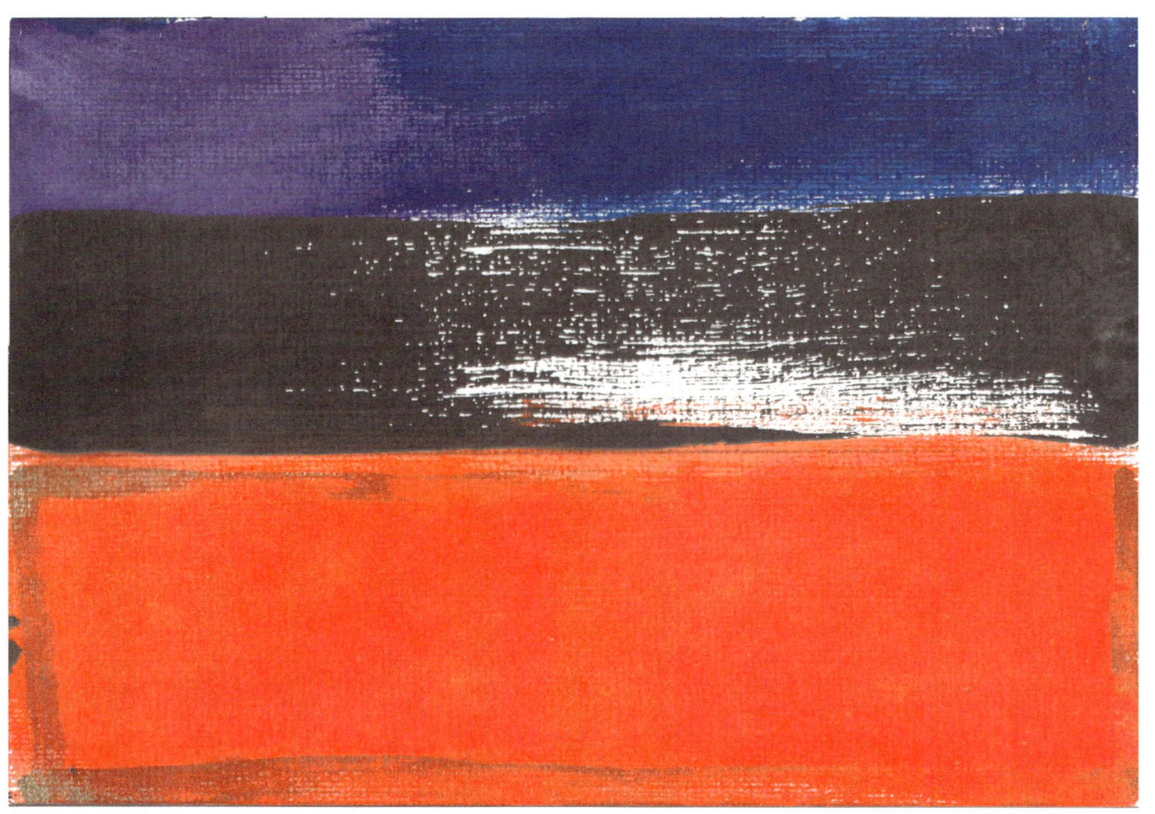

ink & pencil (Dieppe)

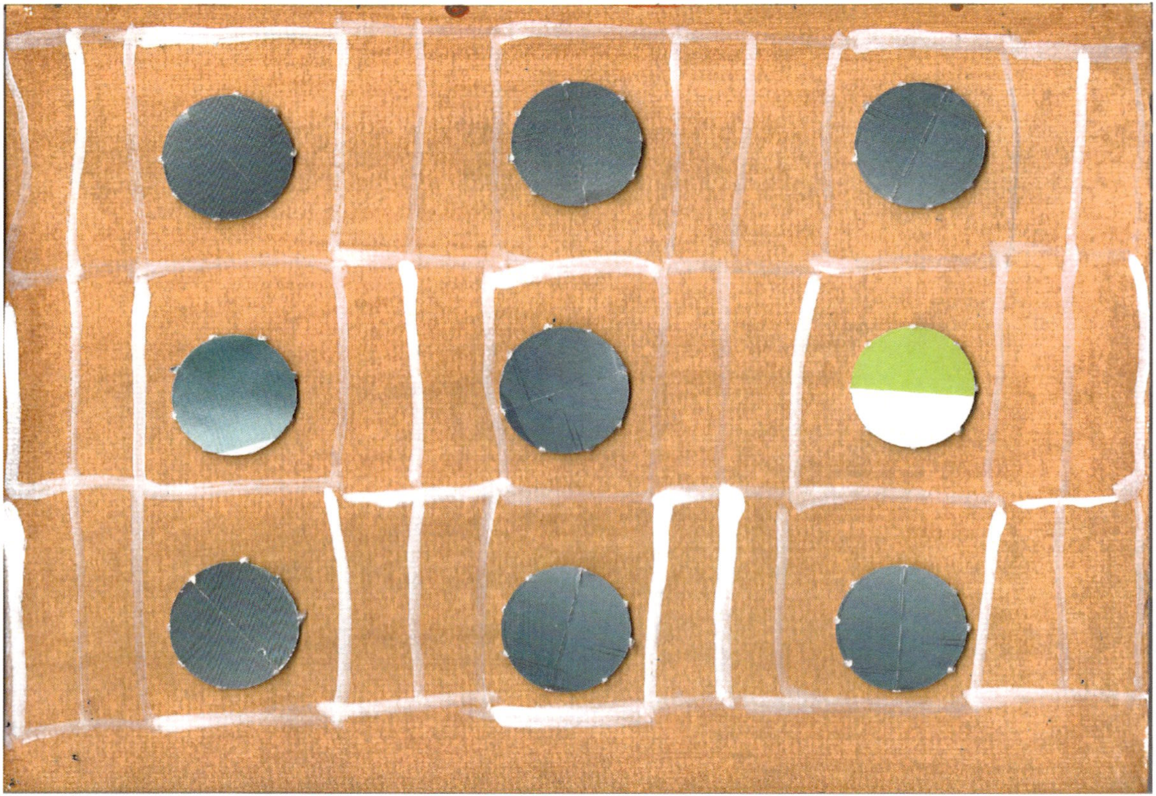

 ink & collage (garden)

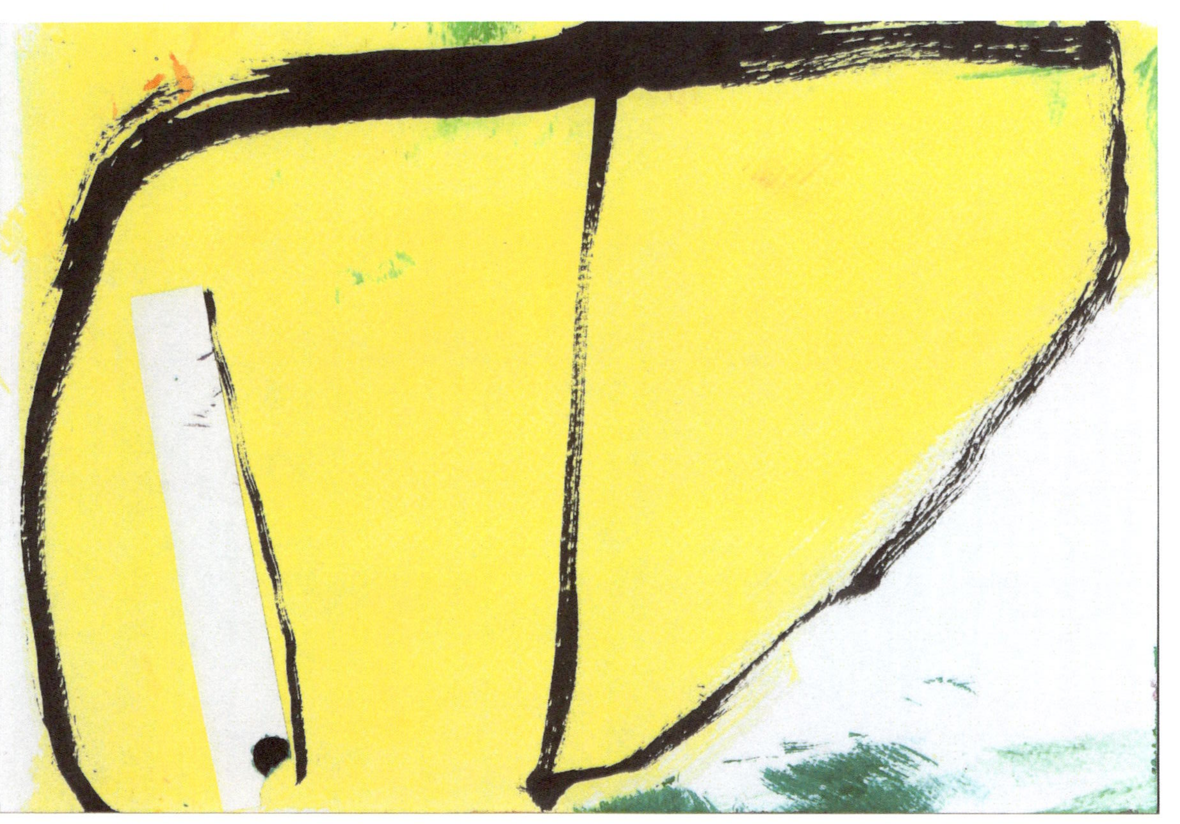

ink & collage (study for Willi Baumeister)

 ink & pencil (for an end to winter)

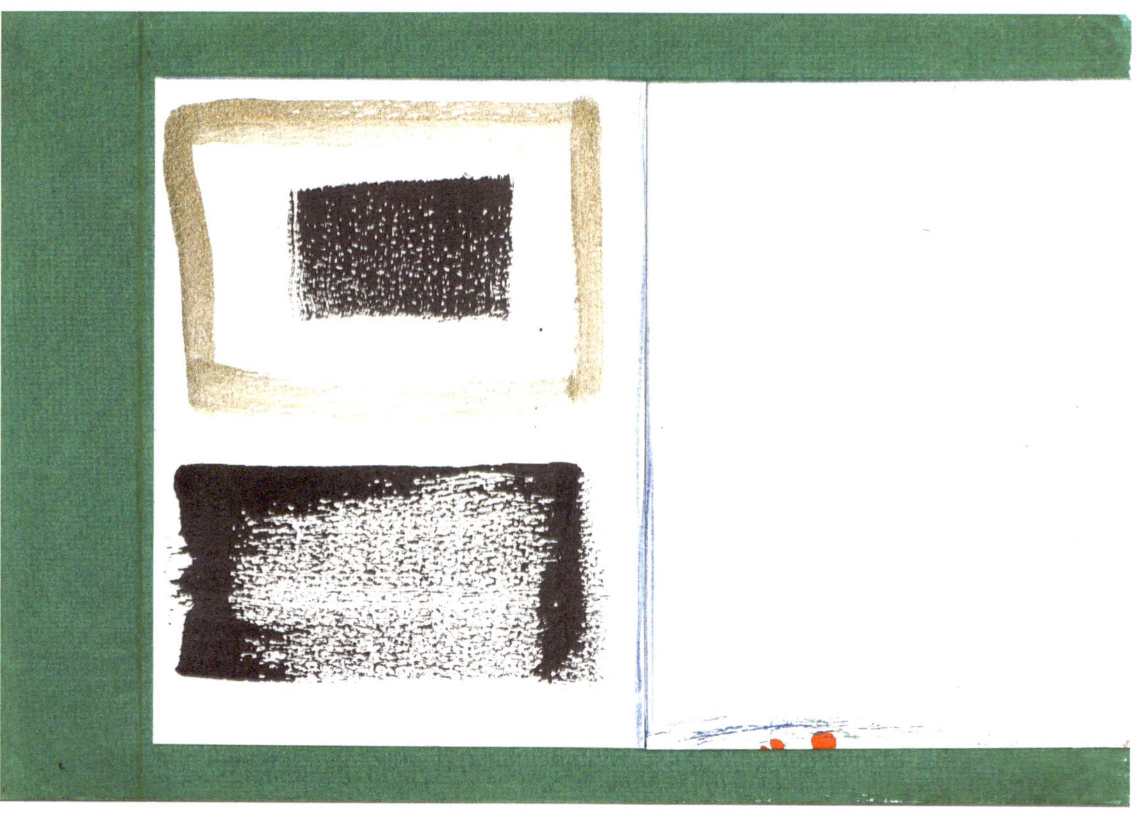

ink & pencil (panels)

David Miller

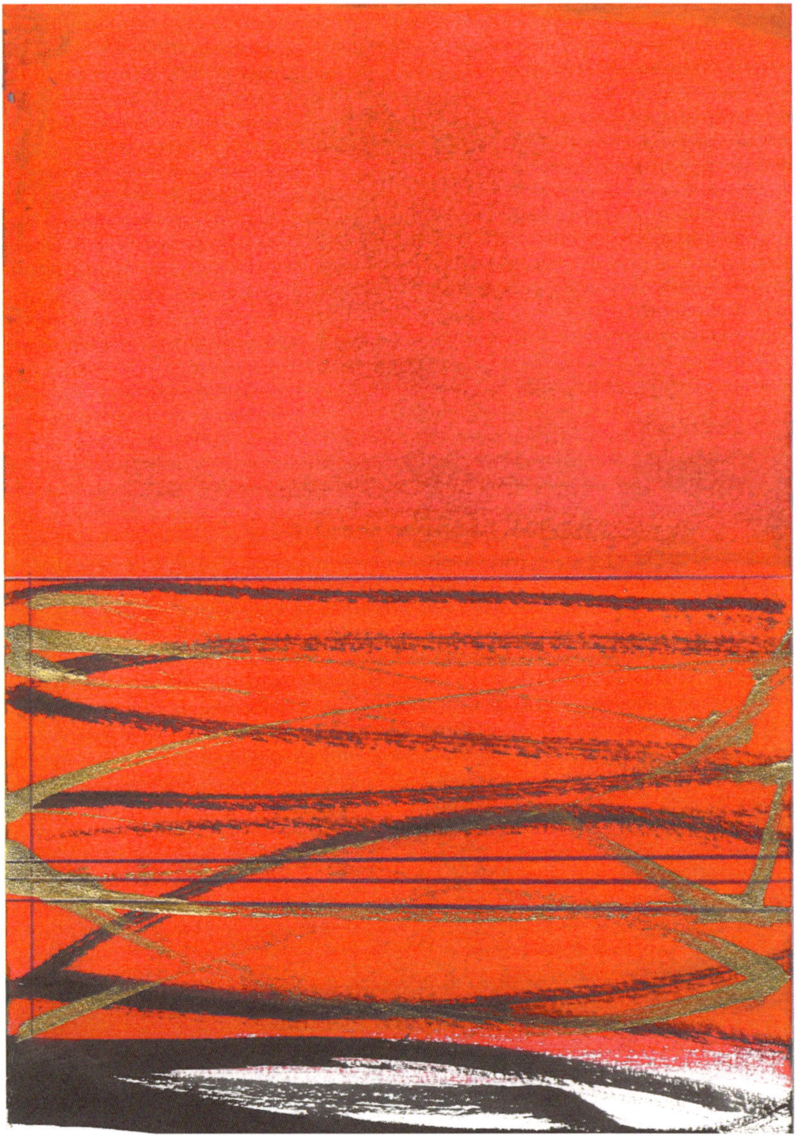

20 | ink & pencil (lucky day)

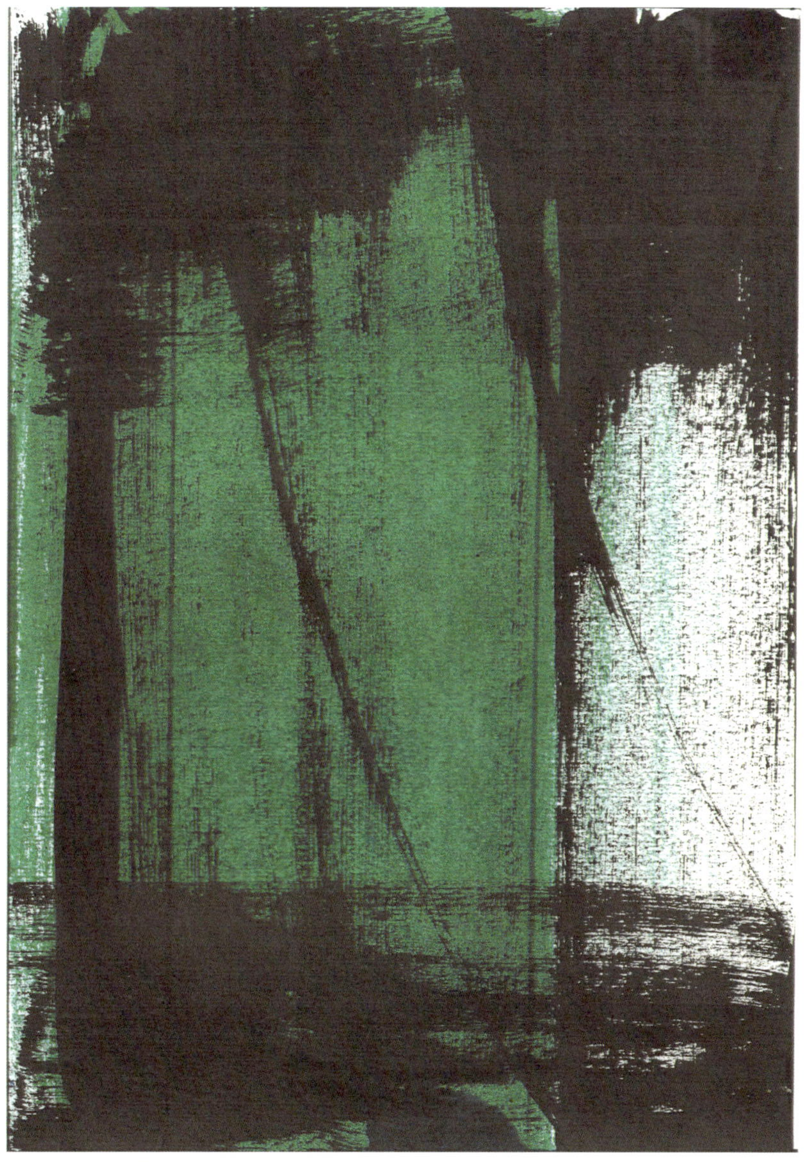

ink & pencil (in memory of Tom Lowenstein)

 ink & pencil (the sign & the shadow)

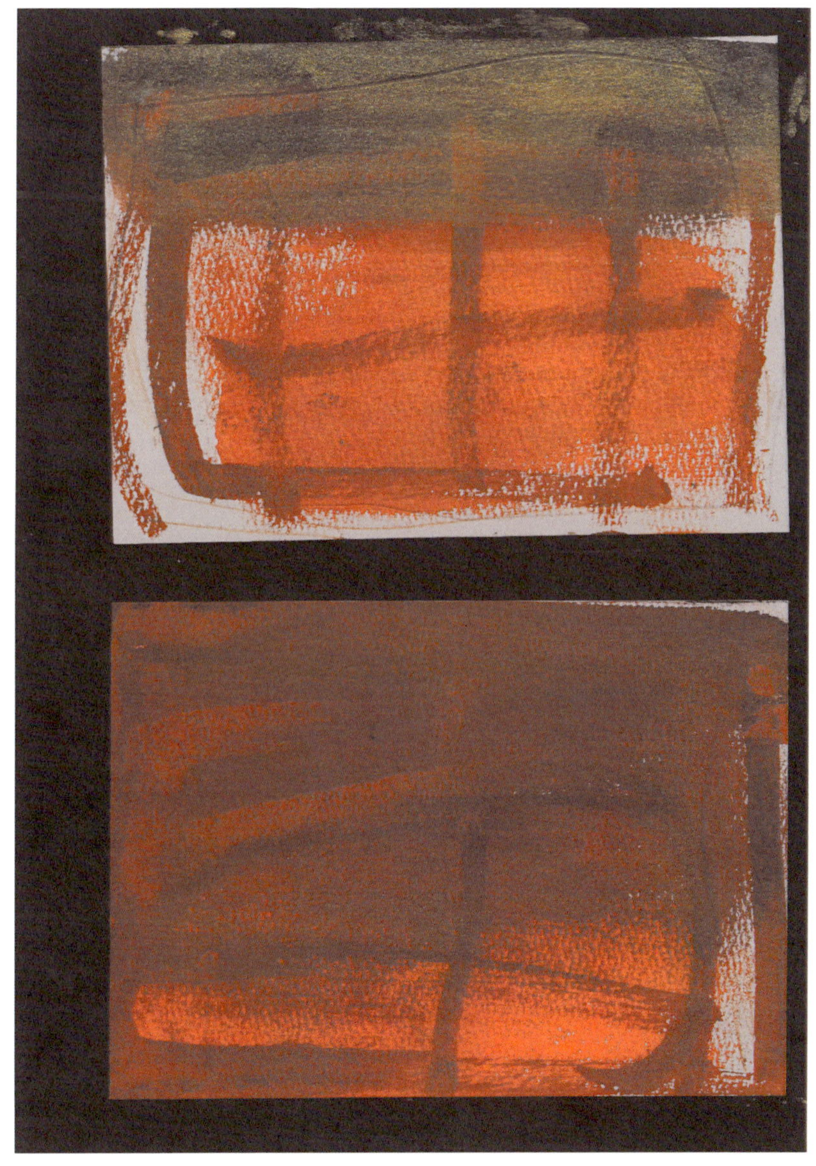

ink & pencil (panels)

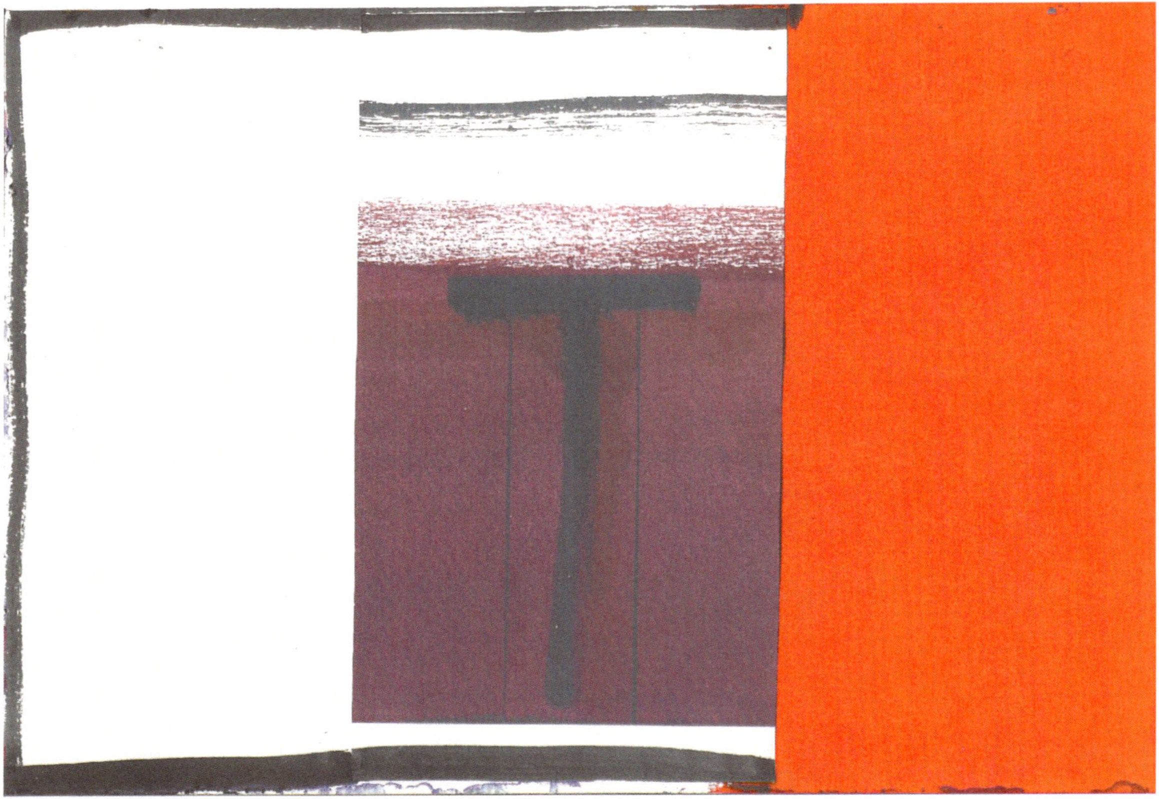

 ink & photocopy (the sign & the stain)

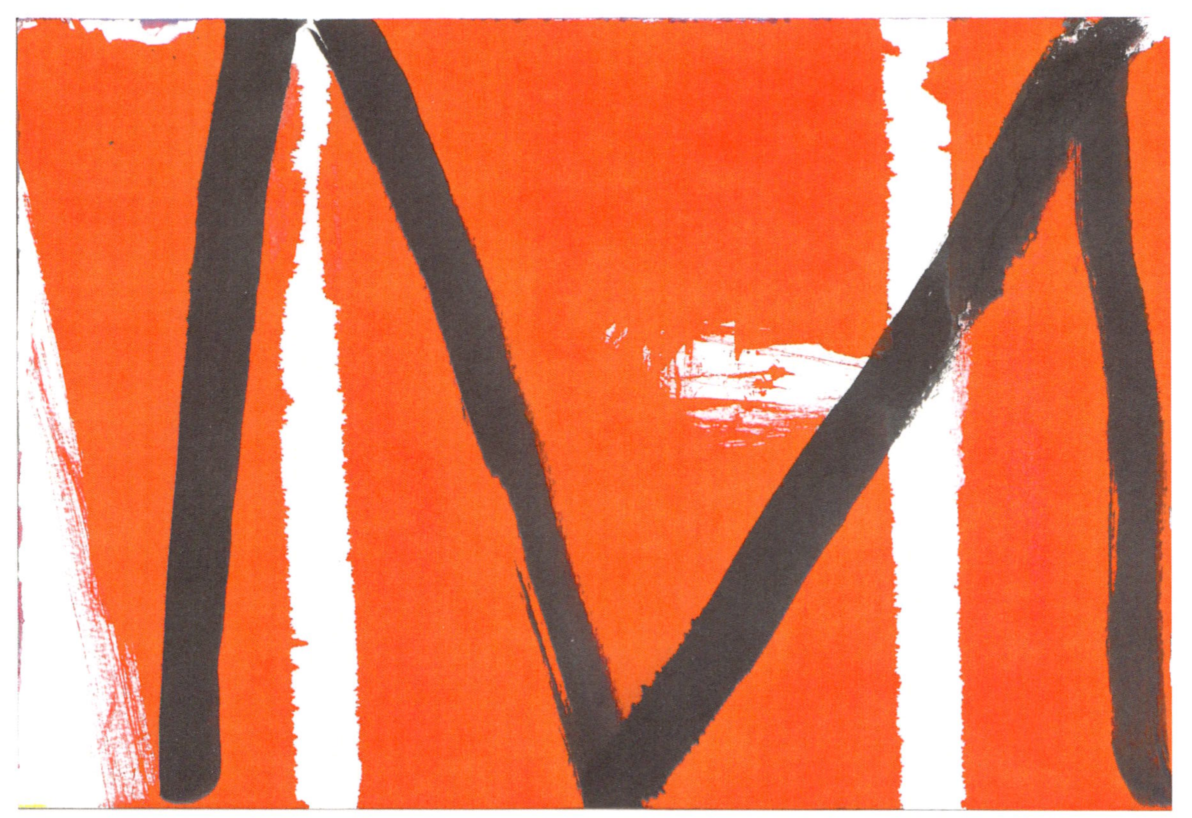

ink (black white red)

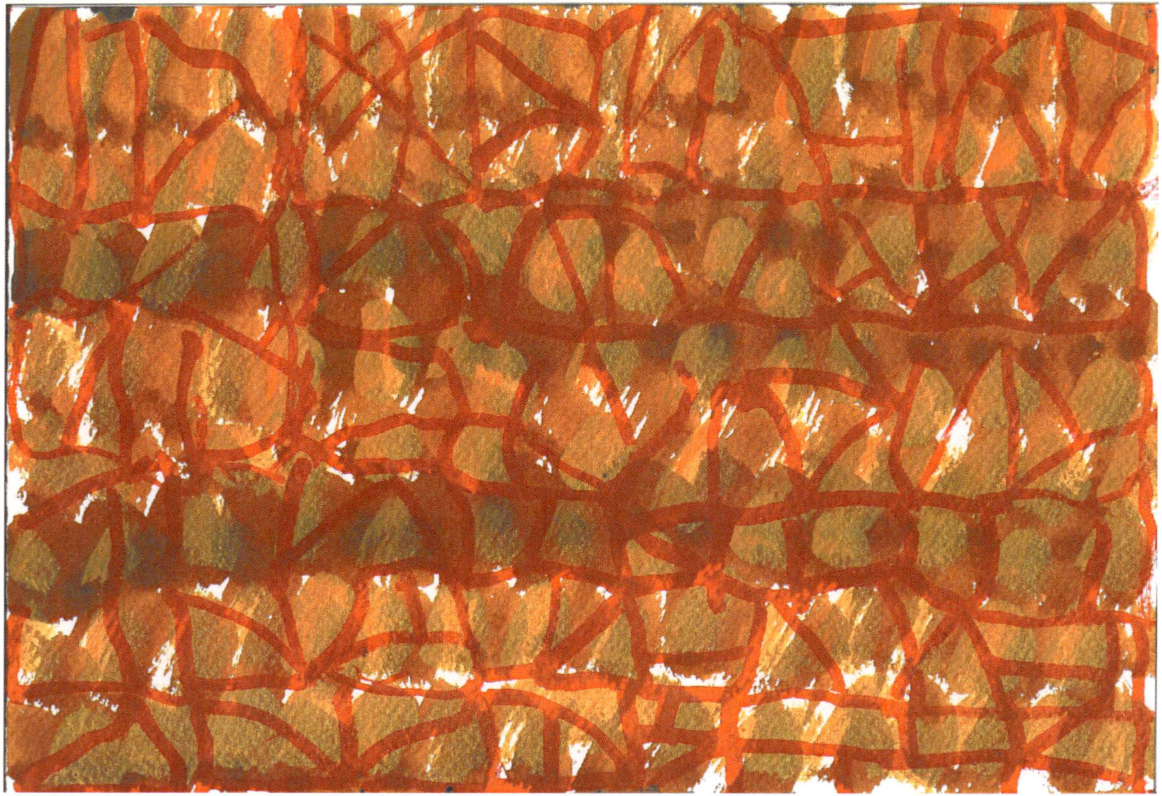

26 | ink (as if it were autumn)

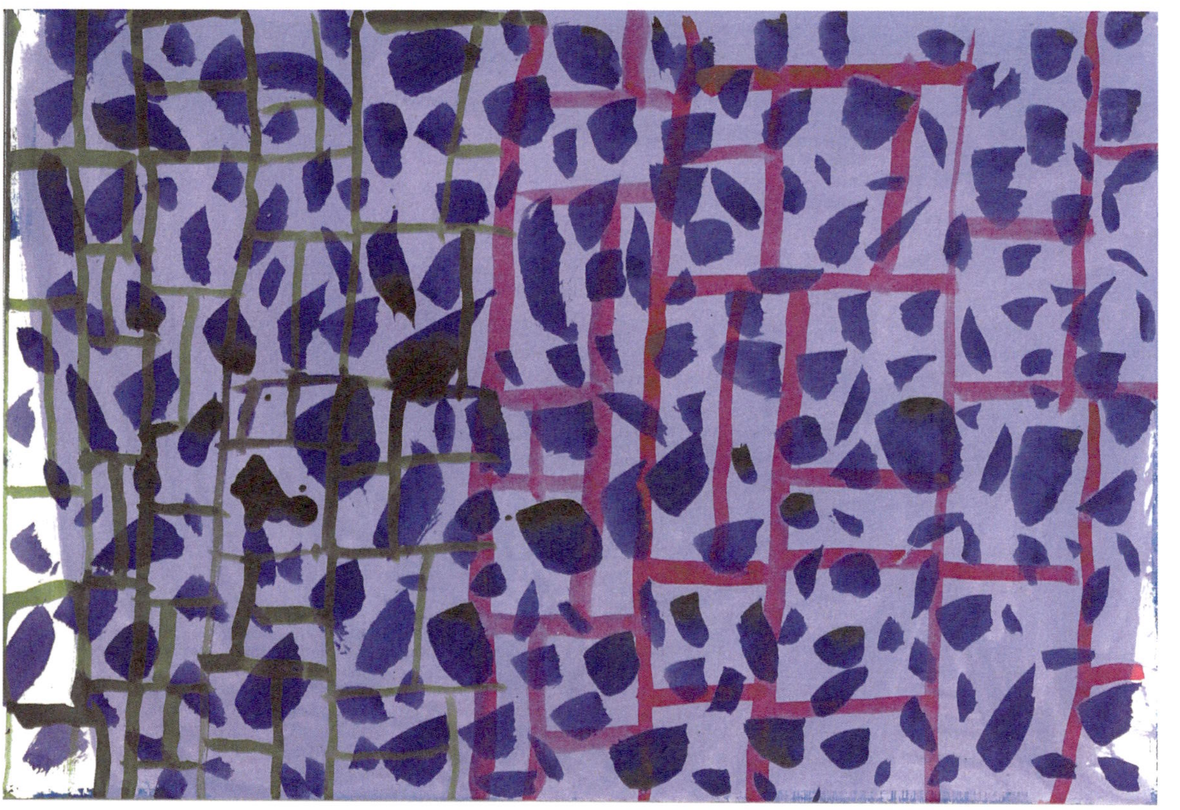

ink (Dodo's birthday)

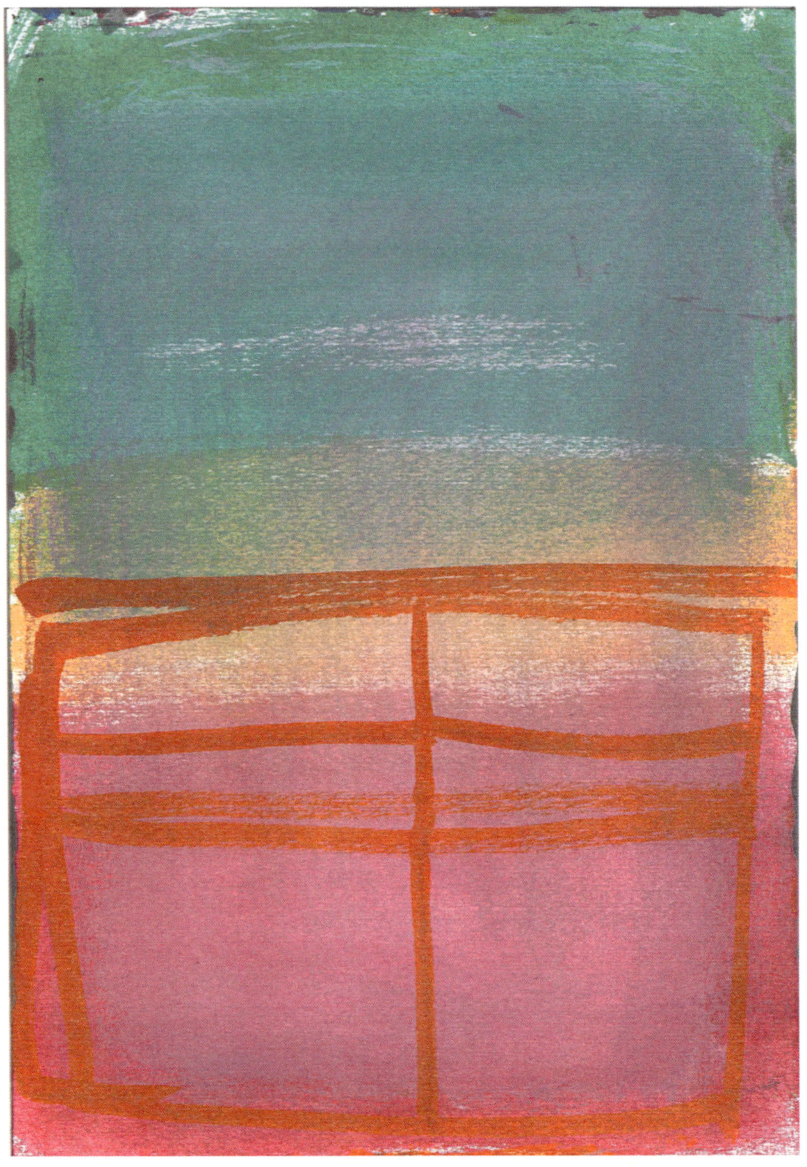

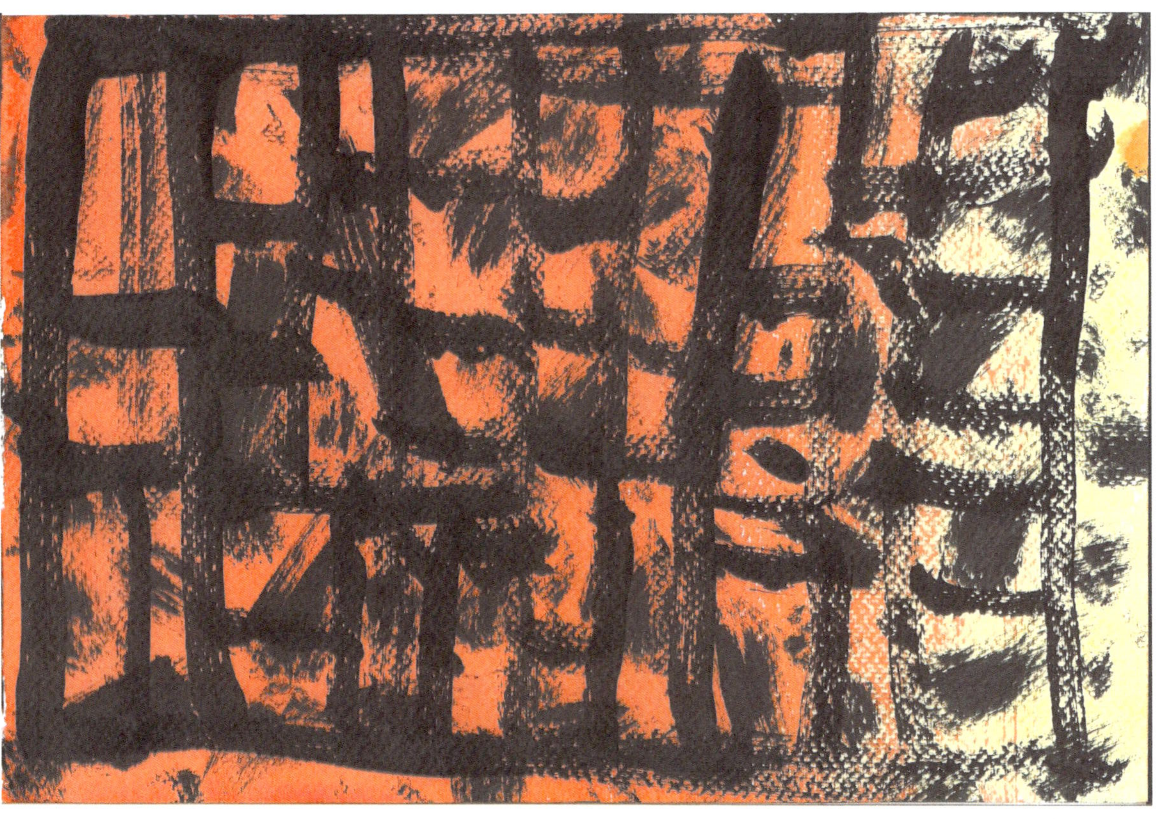

ink (grille)

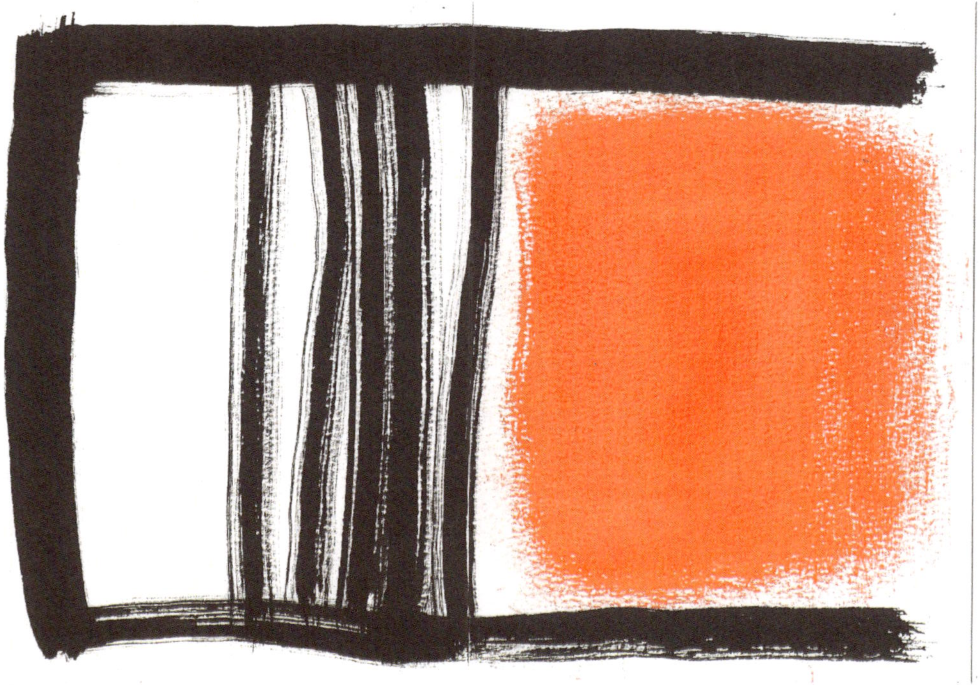

30 | ink (black orange white)

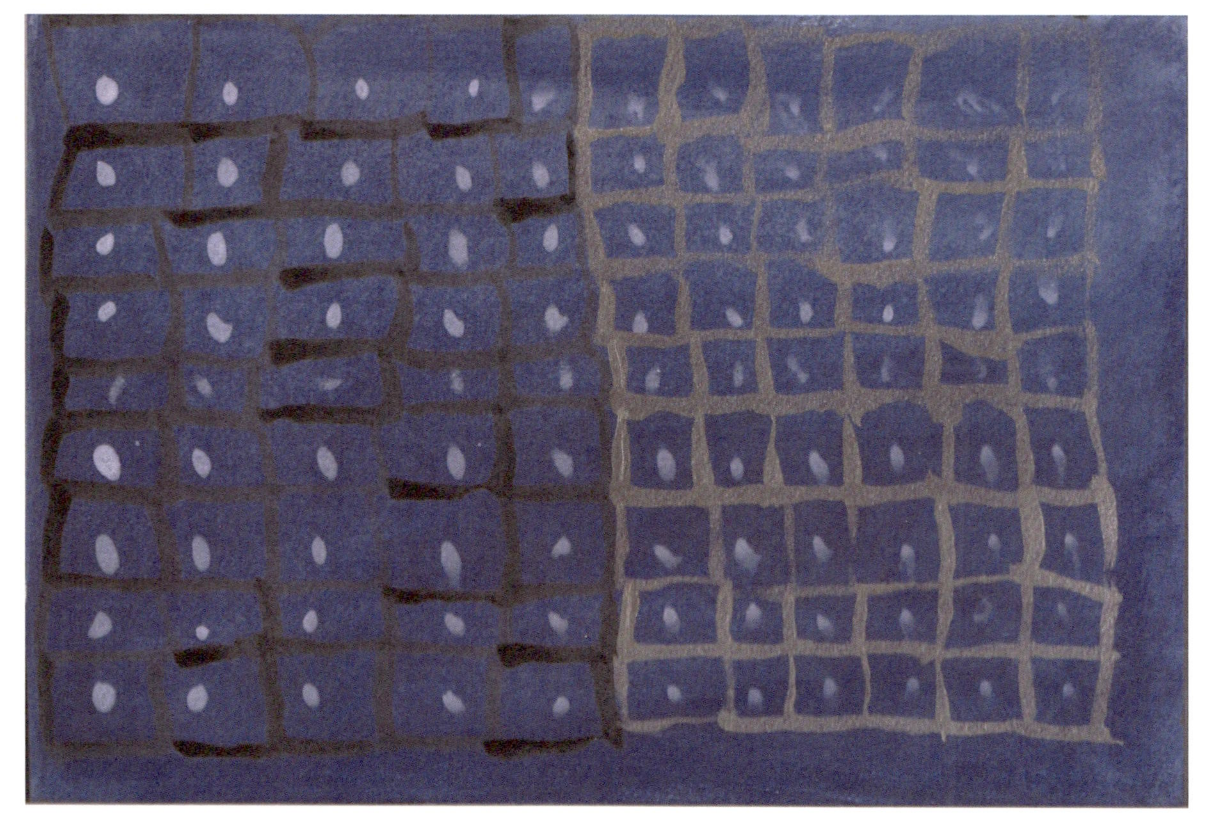

ink (double lattice)

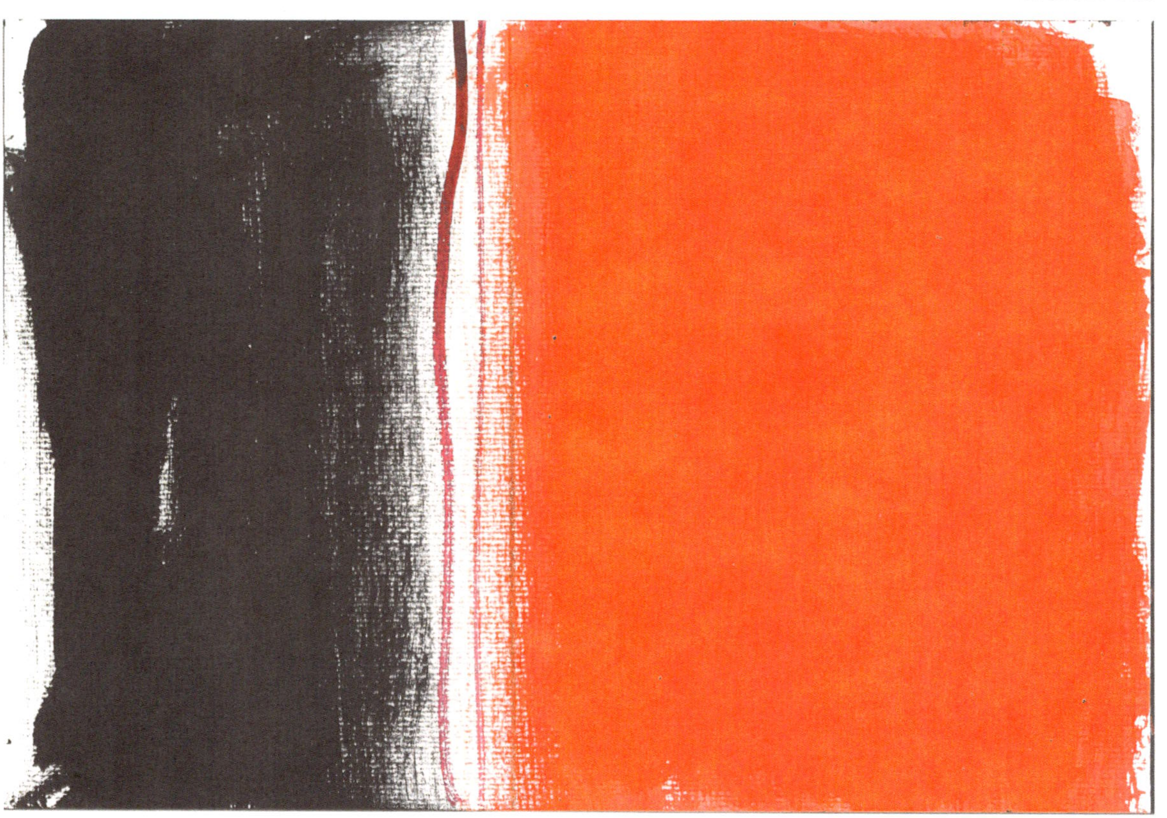

ink & pencil (mostly black & orange)

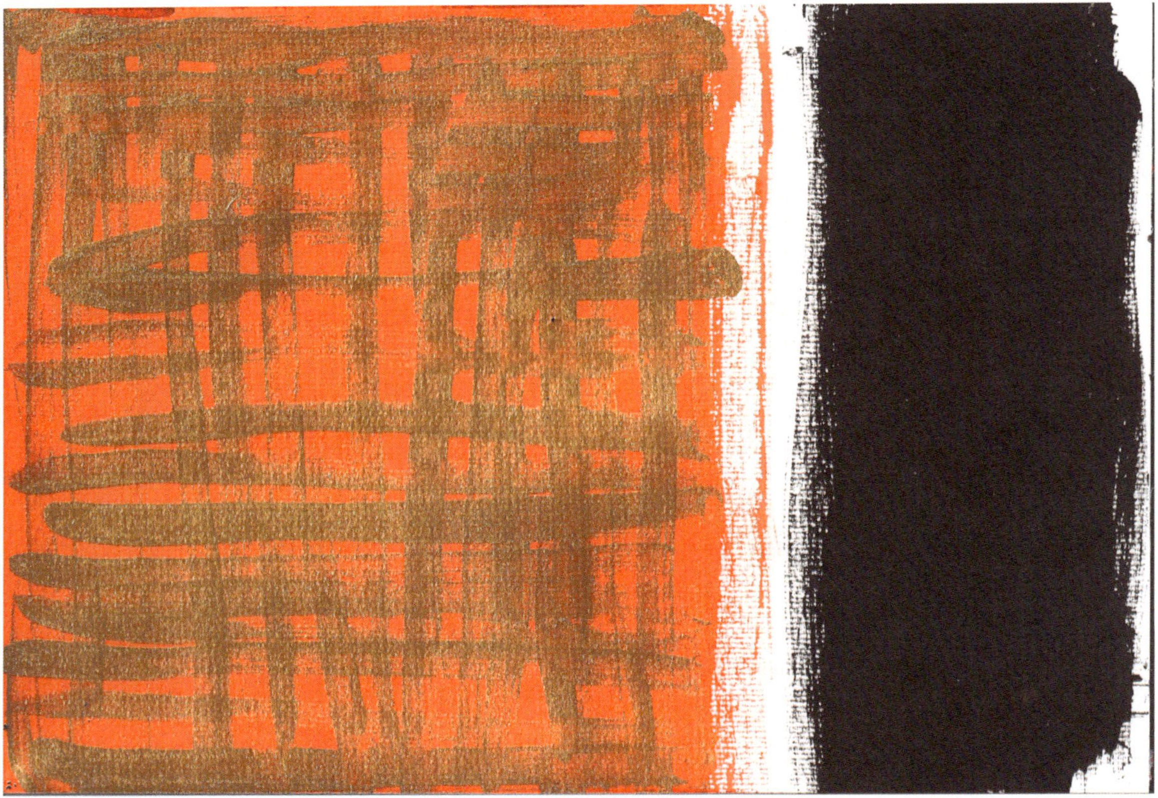

 | ink (message for Mathias Goeritz)

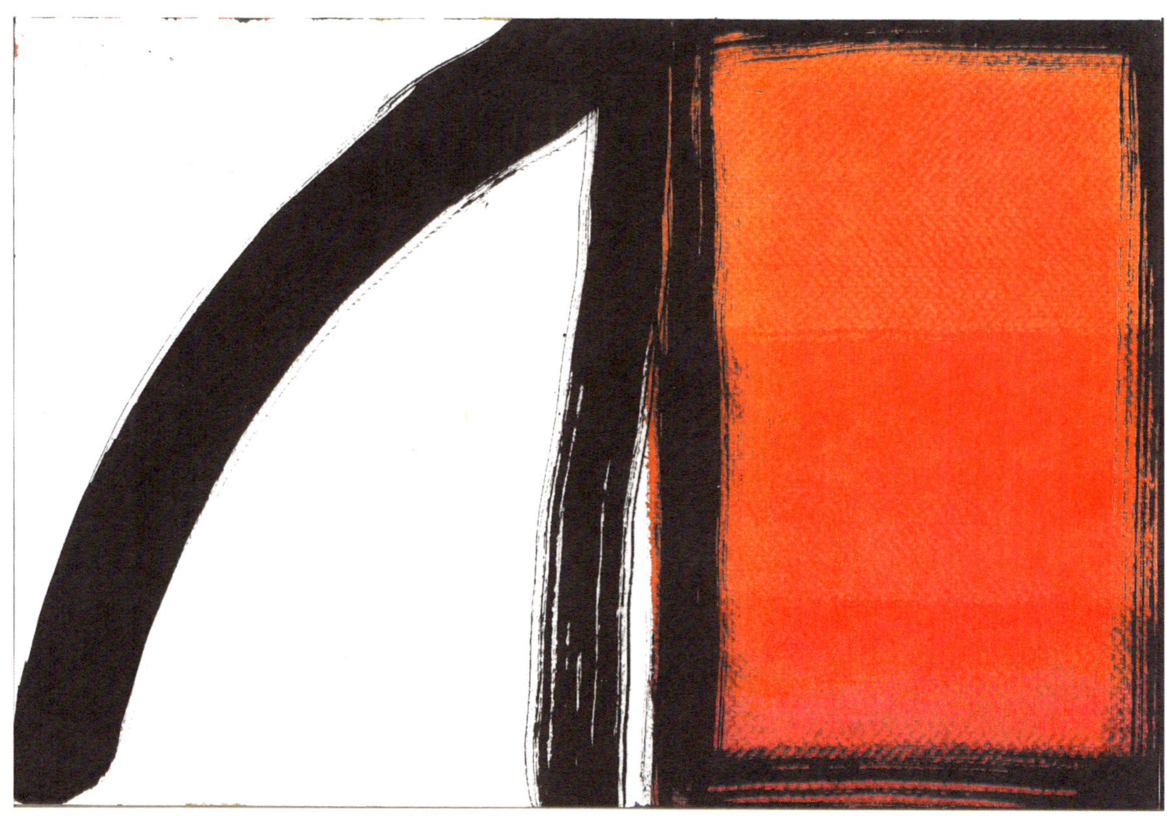

ink (open & enclosed)

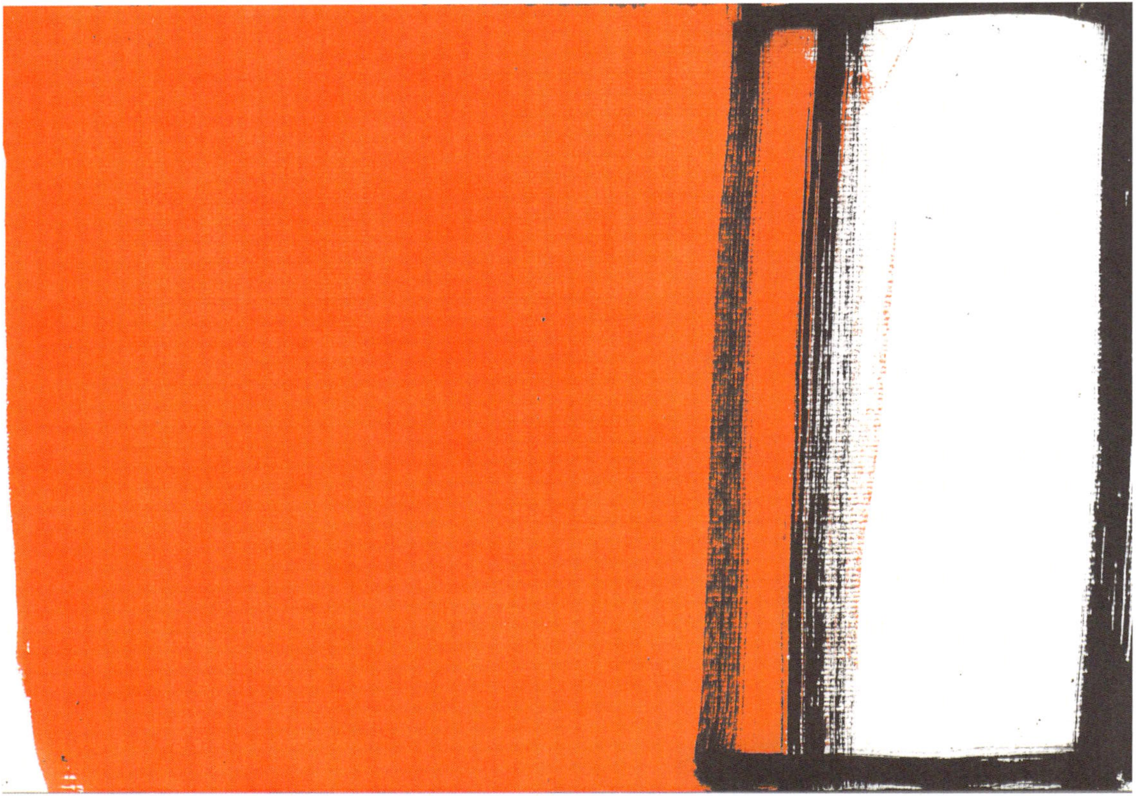

 ink (orange white black)

ink (single brushstroke over colours)

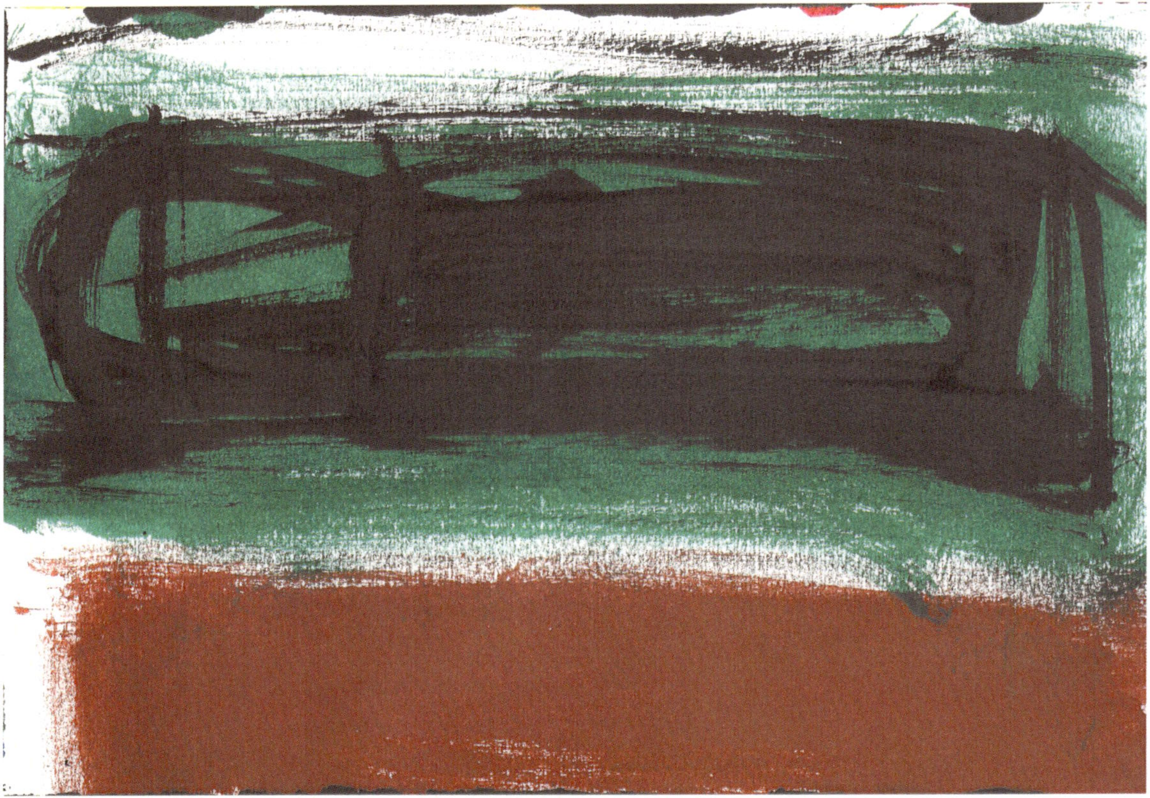

38 | ink (late for Pasmore)

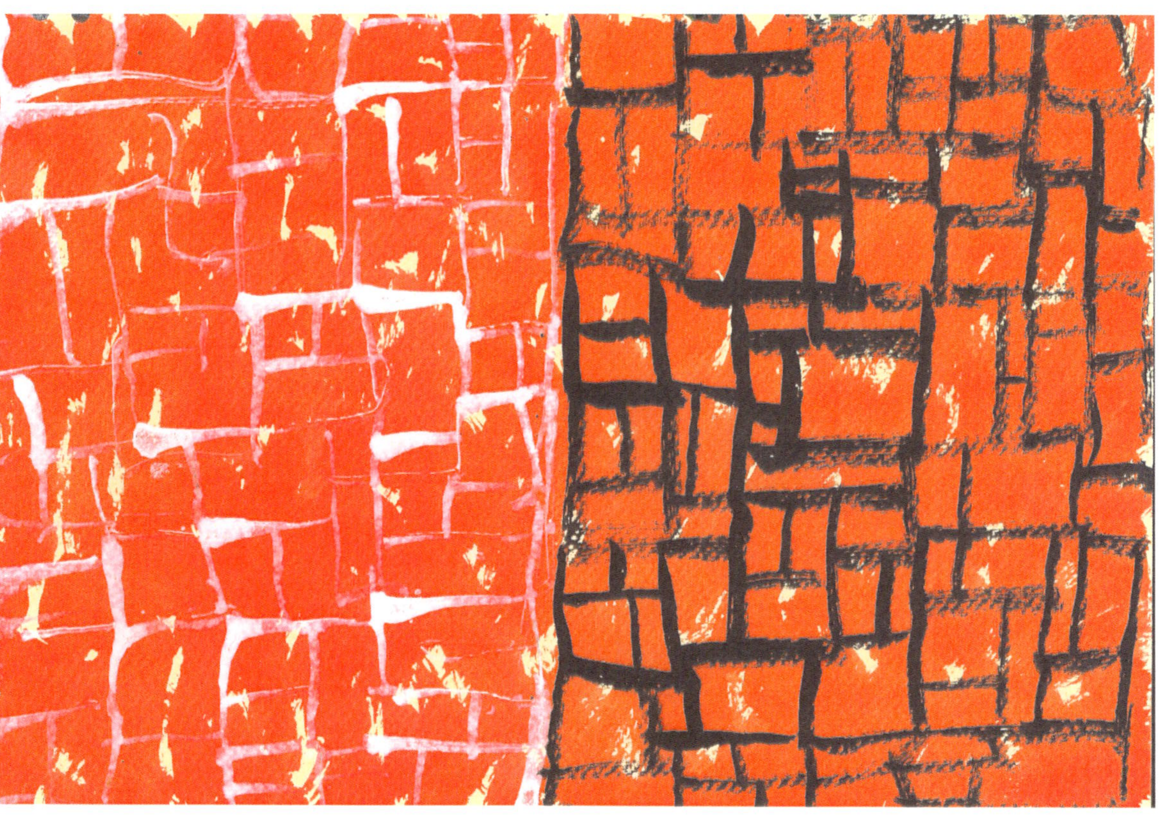

ink (towards Christmas)

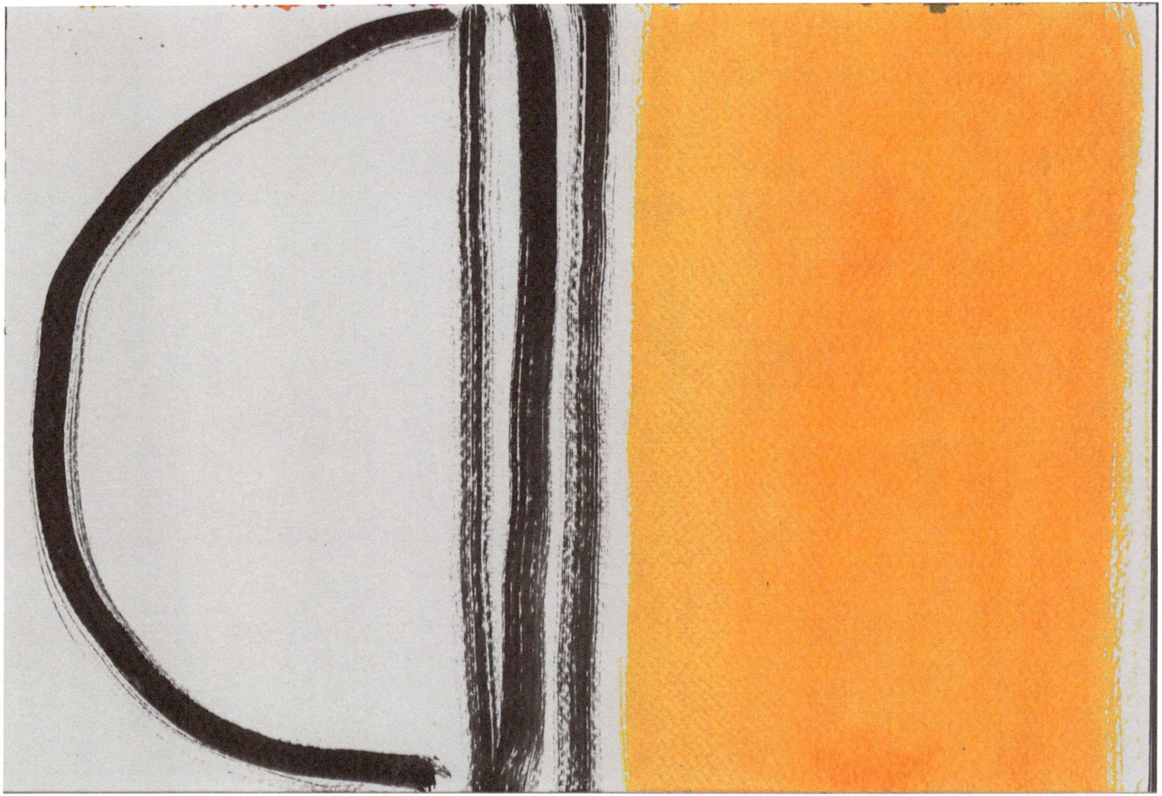

 ink (black yellow white)

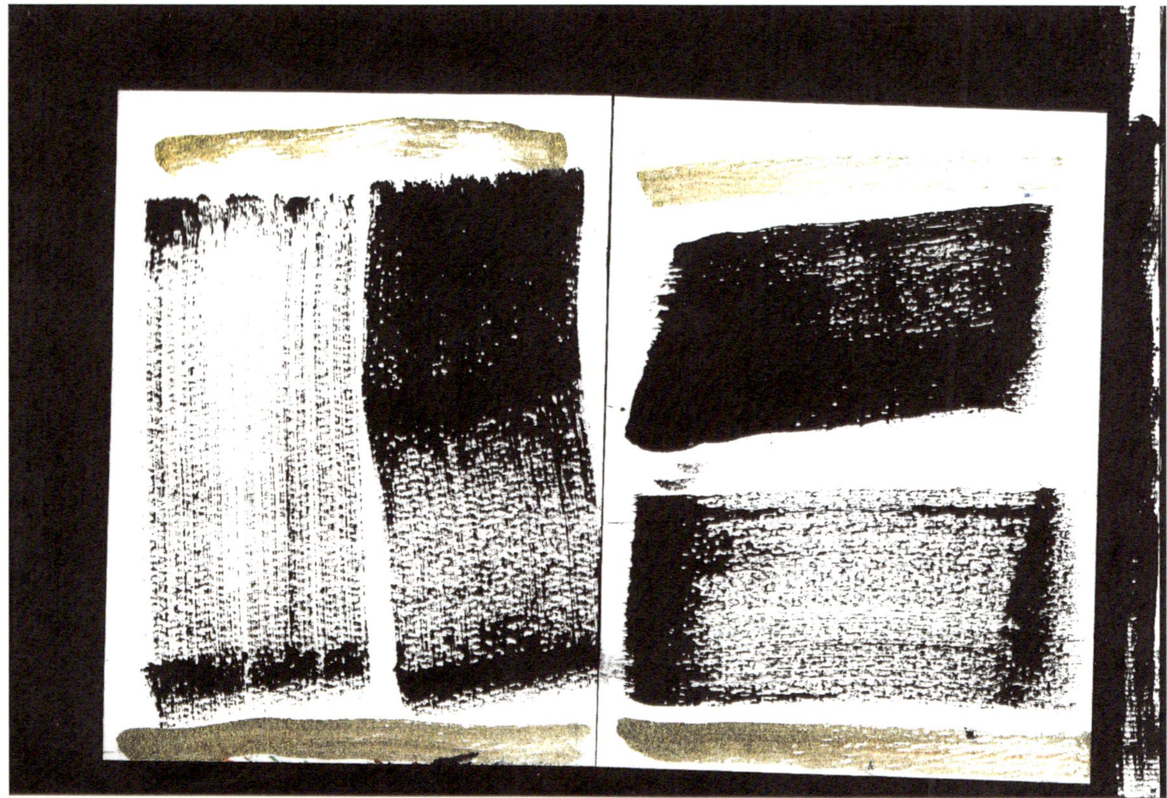

ink (panels) |

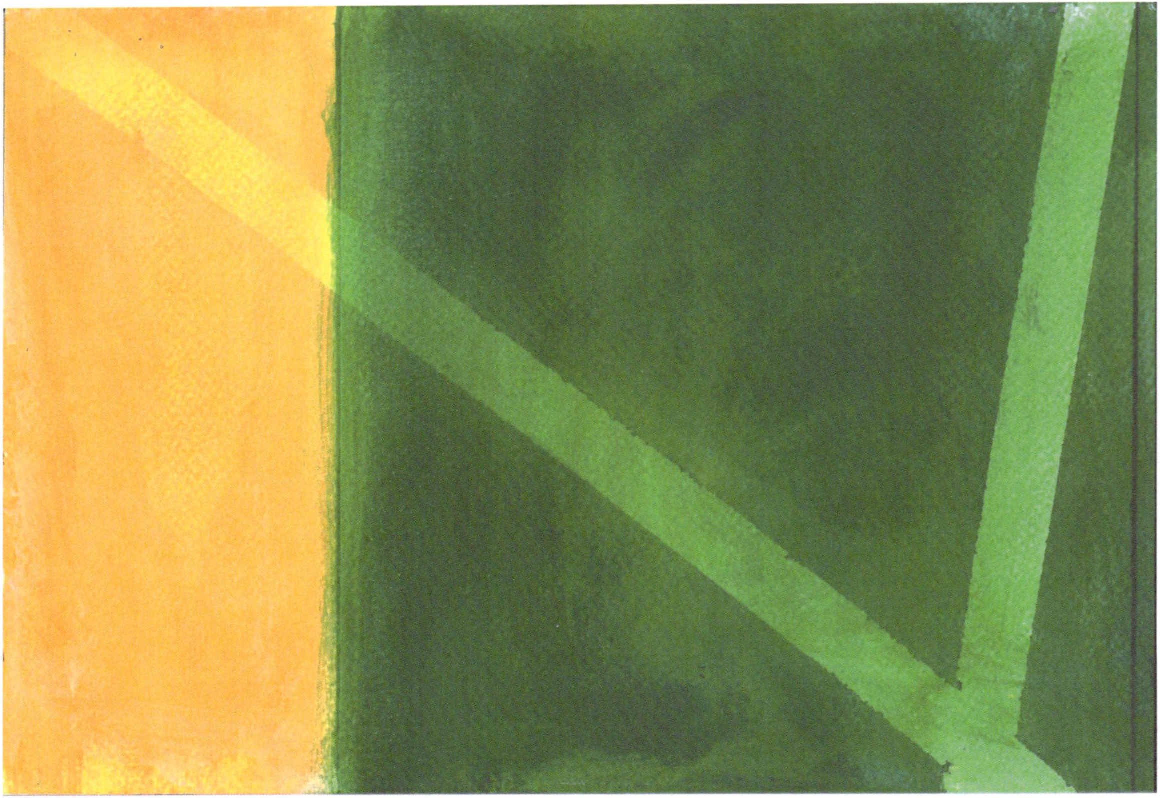

 | ink and pencil (simple piece 2)

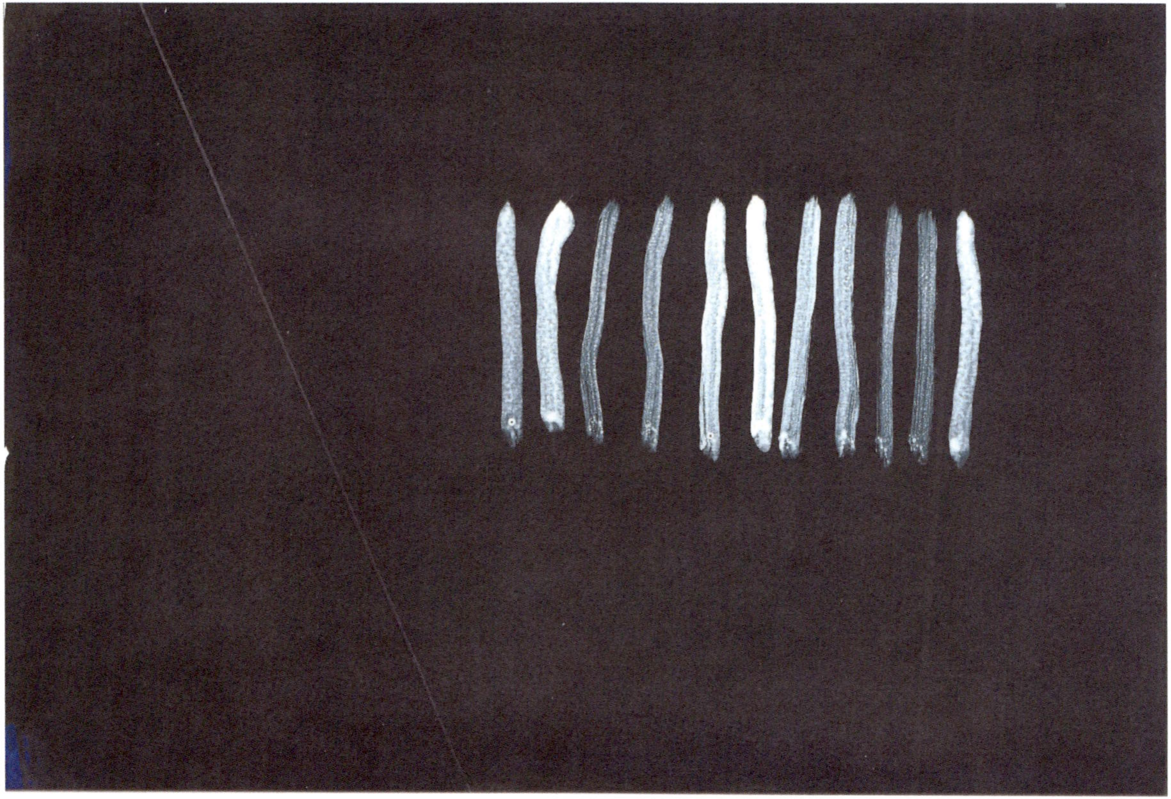

ink and pencil (night in the afternoon)

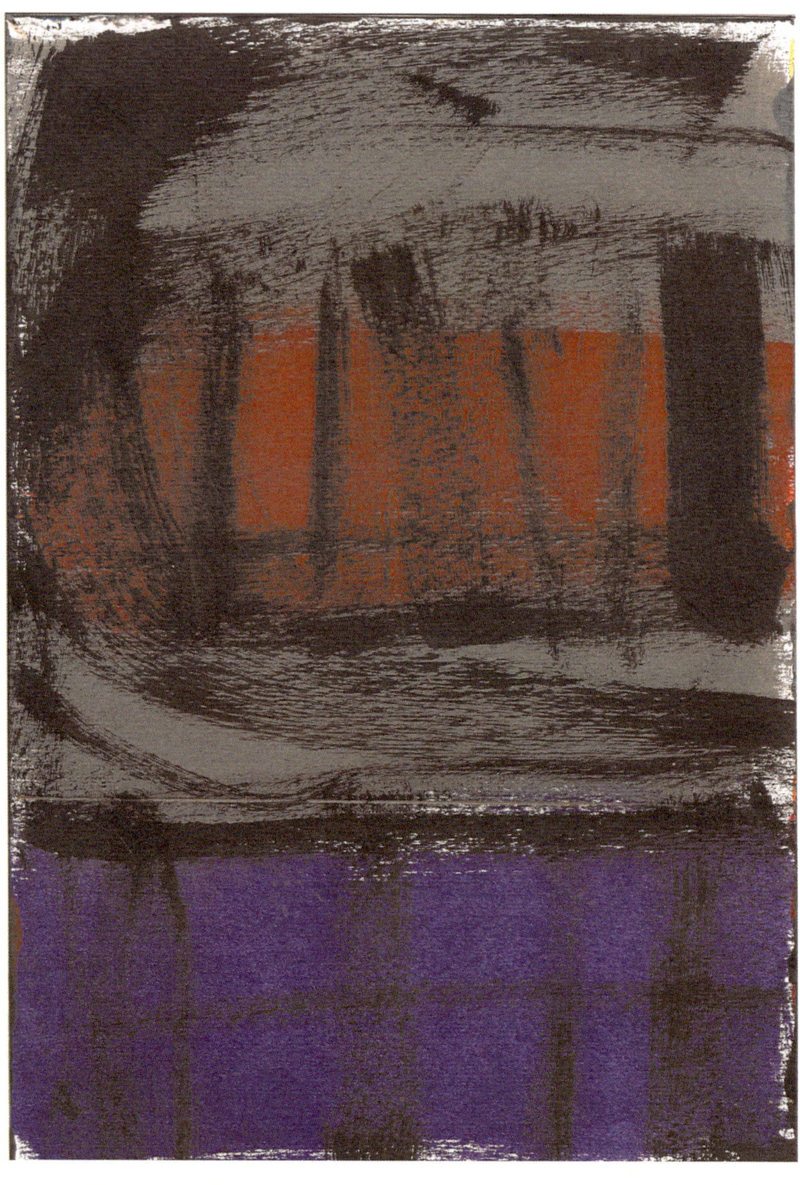

 | ink pencil (Easter)

About the Author

David Miller is a third generation Australian who was born in Melbourne in 1950, but who has lived in the UK since 1972 – first in London and then in Bridport (Dorset). His art has appeared on the covers of books by Fanny Howe, Robert Lax, Isadore Lhevinne and Peter Barry, as well as books of his own from Knives Forks and Spoons Press and Spuyten Duyvil Publishing. He has published visual books, and books including visuals, from tel-let publications, Runaway Spoon Press, Veer Publications and Knives Forks and Spoons Press, and has shown his work in group exhibitions in London and Cornwall. In addition, his visual work has appeared in such journals as *BlazeVOX, ETC, Golden Handcuffs Review* and *Poetry Salzburg Review.* He is also a musician and a member of the Frog Peak Music collective.

www.ingramcontent.com/pod-product-compliance
Lightning Source LLC
LaVergne TN
LVRC080922110826
845147LV00025B/742

* 9 7 8 1 9 1 6 5 9 0 1 8 2 *